BUILDING A
TENNIS
CHAMPION

BUILDING A
TENNIS
CHAMPION

By Nathan and Giselle Martin

30 Things Every Tennis Player, Coach and Parent Must Know

http://tennisfitness.com/online-tennis-programs/

ISBN: 978-14943974-6-3

1

To our beautiful children;
Jacob and Jacinta.

May you continually learn and
strive to be your best.

PREFACE

We decided to write this book after constantly being asked the same questions by tennis coaches, parents and young players. We wanted to share some insight and experience on what it takes to build a tennis champion. If you are involved with a young tennis player's development, there is a good chance the topics covered in this book may be questions you, yourself, may want to know. We are glad to share some of our knowledge and we hope you get the answers you are looking for.

Nathan and Giselle

ABOUT THE AUTHORS

Proud Australians, Nathan and Giselle Martin have worked as Tennis Fitness Trainers for over 15 years. Collectively, they have trained 5 former world number 1 players. Living in Australia, they have frequently travelled on the WTA and ATP tours, assisting the world's top Professionals. When in Australia, Nathan, Giselle and their team at Tennis Fitness, have a strong connection with developing junior tennis players; continually sharing their knowledge and experience with potential future Professionals. Their passion to continually learn and share about the game they love has led them to become world leaders in the tennis industry.

Nathan and Giselle have worked with Lleyton Hewitt, Martina Navratilova, Casey Dellacqua, Sam Stosur, Svetlana Kuznetsova, Arantxa Sanchez Vicario, and Monica Seles.

INTRODUCTION

If you're a young tennis player, tennis coach or tennis parent, this book is a must read. "Building a Champion" covers a diverse range of questions regarding young tennis players. If you have ever asked yourself any of these questions, then this book should be in your hands ASAP.

- How often should a young tennis player practice, train and play?
- What off court training should a young tennis player do to improve their game?
- What to eat, before, during and after training/ matches?
- How to keep a young player motivated and focused.
- Secrets for developing a tennis champion from the Professionals

If you are involved with a young tennis player's development, there is a good chance the topics covered in this book may be questions you, yourself may want to know. In this book we wanted to share some insight and some of our first hand experiences on what it takes to build a tennis champion. This is the first time we are bringing the knowledge from the Professionals and making it available to you.

There are a lot of factors to take in to consideration when working with young players. The focus of this book is to help educate everyone involved in a young player's development. Whether it is their physical tennis condition, keeping them emotionally balanced, or their nutrition, gaining practical knowledge and applying it, will give them the edge. If you want to look back and say you have done everything you could for your young player/s, then this book is a good place to start.

Contents

ACKNOWLEDGMENTS

Perhaps you have a child, or maybe it's you, with some natural tennis talent and a desire to be the best tennis player you can be. This book explains all you need to know about fostering tennis talent, from the team of professionals you need to work with to grow that talent to the correct nutrition and programs to follow; even tips on goal development, time management and budgeting considerations.

If you think you know someone who could be the next Lleyton Hewitt, then this is the book for you. We invite you to follow us through the steps taken to maximise the talent you can see; to be the best tennis player you are capable of being and recognising ultimate success.

1. Why Building a Network of Professionals is so Important?

Professionals; qualified people in their respective field (coaches, trainers, doctors, physiotherapists, podiatrists, massage therapists etc.), are always learning, always pushing the boundaries and always adapting their skills, based on latest research. They do what they do for a reason; because they love it and the longer they have been in it, generally, the better they become. They have focused their training and education on a particular area of expertise and have developed knowledge and experience that comes with time.

Providing your child with a professional network is like covering all your bases as best you can. Injuries can ruin a child's tennis future and most of the time, they can be prevented. Having regular assessments by a physiotherapist, trainer, podiatrist etc. will aid in injury prevention by allowing the professional the opportunity to pick up certain things before they worsen or eventuate. We know a few professional players, who have made it with zero to little support from a network, but it has been extremely tough and if they could do it again with a solid network, they would. We are not saying to go out and spend $1000's of dollars on your child weekly or monthly for no reason, but apart from the investment in a tennis coach for your child, invest in regular checkups and if needed, get assistance from the professional in that field.

Here is what we recommend as your professional network, apart from tennis coaching, as a basic guideline for a child's well being, physical development and injury prevention;

1. **Me·** Weekly to quarterly sessions with a tennis fitness trainer, see page 5 for role description. A trainer will cost $50-$150 per session individually, or less if in groups. A specific tennis trainer should be able to provide a program that can be followed for up to 8 weeks away from the trainer, making it cost effective.

2. **NHS** Annual consult/checkup with a podiatrist (foot specialist). On average, this costs $100-$250. Additional costs may be required e.g. for orthotics etc.

3. Quarterly consult / checkup with a physiotherapist (body specialist). This will cost $60-$120; you will be able to get specific programming for injury prevention etc. included in the consult fee.

4. **Me·** Monthly massage therapist providing manual release of muscle tension from the body and costs $50-$150. A sports massage therapist is preferable.

5. **Me·** Annual or every 2 years Sports Nutritionist consult to assess eating / fluid habits and give recommendations and food guidelines specific for the individual. A Sports Nutritionist will start to educate young players on correct eating habits which, in our opinion, is critical for their future health. This will cost $100-$300, and should include a food guidelines/eating plan).

Other professionals who play a role are:

1. Sports doctor, if a major or long term injury occurs.

2. Sports psychologists. We highly recommend 3-6 sessions with a sports psychologist to give young players an insight into competing, dealing with expectations and pressure, strategies for staying focused and remaining calm whilst practising and competing.

Note: Some of these expenses will partly be covered by private health funds.

1.1 Role of the tennis coach

A coach should provide their tennis players with the expertise and knowledge to improve their tennis game, in a safe and healthy environment. The coach controls a large part of the player's development, as they are responsible for:

1. Technical advice
2. Motivation
3. Tennis related goal setting
4. Tournament selection
5. Providing a network of professionals (Fitness trainers, Physiotherapists, Sports doctors, Nutritionists, Podiatrists etc.)

6. Equipment advice (racquet selection, shoes, clothing, stringing tension)

7. Enforcing good tennis etiquette

8. Competition education (strategies etc.)

A coach's role covers many areas, and along with the parent, are the most critical part of a child's development and their future in the game. They should be involved in major decisions related to the player's tennis. If the child does not feel comfortable, motivated or challenged enough with their coach, then that should be communicated to the coach.

1.2 Role of the tennis parent

The role of the tennis parent is to "facilitate an environment that will foster enjoyment and encourage constant growth". This means providing care and support for a child and placing them in the right environment. Included in this is:

1. Keeping the child's needs as a priority (clothing, food, hydration, equipment).

2. Giving positive feedback ("You really look like you are enjoying your tennis", "You did some really good things today", and "It is great to see you are sticking with this").

3. Asking questions ("Are you enjoying your tennis?", "How are you feeling?", "Do you feel comfortable in this environment?").

4. Finding the right team (coach, trainer etc.).

5. Help make tennis fun and challenging.

6. Provide safe transport to and from matches and practice.

7. Keeping them socially active (tennis is an individual sport; away from the game, keep them socially active with other children).

8. Be a listening board for your child; listen with intent and be open to the child's needs, not what you want to hear.

9. Keep everybody accountable; the majority of the time, the parent is paying for services and they have a right to hold those professionals accountable. Ask questions at the right time; be honest with those involved).

10. Reinforce the message the coach and team are saying. If you want to enable your child to succeed, you need to create an environment where the coach or team member has the reins in their appropriate skill area) The moment the parents take the reins and go over the top of the coach or team member, is the moment boundaries have been crossed and will not only affect the team environment, but the development of the child).

11. Set the example: be on time, keep it positive, be respectful to other parents and children and do not undermine others, especially the child's team, around your child.

1.3 Role of the fitness trainer

The role of the tennis trainer is to "provide the right advice and implement the correct training techniques to aid in injury prevention and improve the strength and tennis conditioning of the child". Living in this day and age, it is not only important, but also essential, to have your child doing complimentary exercise away from the tennis court. Tennis skills are now not enough to build a career on; if you are not doing some form of training away from tennis, it may be detrimental to your child's development. We are not saying this because we are trainers; we are saying this because we see what the Professionals and semi Professionals are doing; it's best to start at a young age to encourage the correct movements, loading patterns and most importantly, create good habits.

A tennis specific trainer should provide your child with the following:

1. Education and instruction on correct exercise technique: squatting, pulling, pushing, jumping etc.

2. Tennis fitness and injury prevention assessment to find strengths and weaknesses and to gauge improvements.

3. Provide adequate programming, whether it is one on one training or a program that the child does away from the trainer (it should be specific for the child's needs)

4. Provide a stretching and muscle release program that can be done at home or after practice/ matches

5. A good line of communication between parents, physiotherapists, coaches etc.

6. Help in the prevention and management of injuries.

7. Provide tennis training periodisation programming. This simply is structuring on and off court training into phases or blocks of time.

For more information on Tennis Fitness and Injury Prevention Assessments please visit http://tennisfitness.com/tennis-fitness-training-and-programing/

The basic phases include:

- Preparation – general and specific
- Competition – pre competition and competition
- Transition – off season

Each phase focuses on different aspects of tennis fitness/ strength and conditioning; cardio endurance, strength, power, speed, agility and recuperation in conjunction with on court work, specific for the phase.

For more information on Periodisation Programming for Tennis visit http://tennisfitness.com/how-can-i-peak -for-my-next-tournament/

2. Goal Setting and How to Set Goals?

Goal setting is one of the most important components of planning out a young player's future. If you want to build a champion, you need to create a plan; goal setting is the first step.

2.1 What is goal setting?

Goal setting involves establishing specific, measurable, achievable, relevant and time-targeted objectives (SMART Goal). Goal setting can be broken down into short term goals – 1-6 months, and long term goals – 6months-3 years. For young players, it is best to keep the goals more short term and make them easily attainable to start with, to build confidence and belief.

2.2 Why is goal setting important?

Here are a number of reasons:

1. Setting realistic goals will give a young player a sense of purpose and drive or motivation; they will have something to aim towards.

2. Goal setting will help keep a young player's network: coach, trainer, physio etc., all working together, towards the same target, keep everyone on the same page, so to speak.

3. Goal setting will enable you to monitor the progress of a young player, make you more conscious of their improvements.

4. Goal setting will help you identify a young player's weakness, where they cannot achieve certain goals for various reasons. You then have the opportunity to target the difficulty and progress.

5. The most important component about goal setting is that it gives young players a great sense of self-confidence when they achieve their goals.

2.3 How is goal setting done?

Goal setting is often skimmed over with little to zero relevance or importance. It is one of the most under valued and under used tools in tennis development. Here is some information on goal setting. When goal setting, I like to use the SMART model. It is practical, effective and gives you the ability to use the same procedures each and every time.

S.M.A.R.T. Goals - Smart Goals are broken down into the following areas.

Specific Measurable Attainable Relevant Time

SPECIFIC: Know exactly what you are shooting for. Here are key elements to consider when working out the specific goal.

When setting the specific goal, work with these points;

Who: Who is involved?

What: What do they want to accomplish?

How: Identify requirements and what is involved.

When: Establish a time frame.

Why: Why is it important, benefits of reaching the goal?

Examples:

General Goal – "I want to improve my serve percentage and hit more aces"

Specific Goal – "I want to improve my first serve percentage by 20%. I will get extra lessons on a Saturday for 1 month, focusing on my serve and practice serving on my own Tuesdays and Thursdays after my regular lessons. I will start this Saturday (15th March) and John (my coach) will track my progress by monitoring my matches and keeping my stats. We will assess my progress on the 15th April. When I achieve this I will have more control over my serve and I will give myself the opportunity to hit more aces"

MEASURABLE: How will you know when you have achieved the goal?

What can be used for measurement? Statistics, percentages, results, progression, feedback, assessments etc. Have a definite means of measurement in place within the goal. In our goal example above we used the 20% increase, it can be measured by monitoring the first serve statistics for comparison.

ATTAINABLE: The goal should not be out of reach, nor below par. A goal should be challenging but reachable. Having attainable goals in place gives great motivation to players as it continually drives them, they know they can achieve it and the challenge motivates them. If it is too easy they will feel less satisfaction and if it is too hard, they may drop confidence and motivation.

When working out if the goal is attainable, here are some questions to consider.

Do they have the time to do?

Are there resources available to do it?

Can they financially afford to do it?

Are they ready to do it?

RELEVANCE: Is the goal relevant to the player and their development?

When you know a players strengths and weaknesses, then you can determine what is most relevant to them. Before setting the goal, it is necessary to discuss the relevance and importance of the goal; this will give clarity and will make the player realise whether or not it is worthwhile. It is good to priorities goals in order of relevance. What is most important for their development?

TIME: A time frame needs to be attached to the goal; otherwise there is no sense of urgency or importance associated with it. The time frame must be realistic.

When – When will the goal be completed by?

It is extremely important to have someone that will monitor and determine whether or not the goal is achieved. Make sure they are aware of the exact goal that has been set in place; they must also know the deadline and their role relating to the situation.

Who – Who will keep them accountable?

Goal setting for tennis should take place between a coach/trainer and player. In the case of young players, the parents should definitely be involved, but not overbearing. Follow the SMART goal model above to formulate goals.

Once goals are established, players should be constantly reminded about them; this gives the player a sense of purpose during training and matches etc. Once a goal has been attempted or a time frame has been reached, it is then necessary to evaluate whether the goal has been reached, then revise or reset the goal and continue the sequence.

We don't recommend heavily rewarding young players for reaching goals. Things like food rewards (MacDonald's etc.) or getting to watch more television at night really isn't the way to go, and in all likelihood, it's not going to help them develop as a player. You are better to offer to arrange a one-off extra session with a coach, a piece of tennis equipment they need, a massage or the opportunity to spend time with friends in a fun environment; organise to take the young player and some of their friends to the cinema.

Remember, set attainable goals, especially initially. It is extremely important to get young players to buy into the process and gain confidence from reaching something they have planned to!

2.4 Discover 10 tips in keeping a young tennis player motivated

1. Get involved and enthusiastic about tennis yourself. Watch matches on TV, follow the professional tours, and plan trips to watch tournaments. Young players take in a lot from

adults; they can feed off our enthusiasm and attitude towards things.

2. Get people around them that they respect: coaches, other players, tennis fitness trainers. If they don't respect their environment, they won't want to be there.

3. Continually remind them of the positive experiences they have had with the sport, whether it was a certain match played, a professional match watched, a tennis trip or training sessions.

4. Set attainable goals. Setting goals they are confident they can achieve, will give them a great sense of drive and determination. (SMART Goals principle).

5. Outsource the motivation by placing young players in a positive environment or with motivated individuals, such as coaches, trainers, players or friends, who will rub off on young players.

6. Remind players that success is achievable with practise, determination and dedication. This must be done in the right way at the right time, not in frustration or anger.

7. Get them watching or reading true sporting stories. This is a great way to produce inspiration and belief that they can do it.

8. Pick up on the positives and focus on them, make note and mention the negatives at the right time.

9. Practise and training should be challenging and enjoyable. Create structure around those two things.

10. The goal of the parent/coach is to help young players practice making good decisions, not to make the decisions for them all the time. When a young player feels they are doing something they have chosen to do, they will be a lot more determined and motivated to get the job done.

Last but not least, parents and coaches who stay positive with words, actions and show patience with young players, have the best chance of seeing the young player's motivation increase and stay there.

It can be challenging at times for parents, coaches and trainers to keep young players motivated. Let's look at some factors that affect motivation and enthusiasm with young players.

1. **Over training or burnout leads to fatigue, mental and physical.** This is caused by training too much or not resting enough. We would say this is one of the main reasons young players lose motivation. It can be avoided by having a structured training plan and monitoring the young player's health and well being. We have developed a player monitoring sheet that we get players to fill out every few days; it helps gauge how they are feeling mentally and physically and gives you the ability to work out the right volume and intensity specifically for them. (Please contact us for more information on the tennis monitoring sheets).

For more information on Tennis Monitoring Sheet please visit http://tennisfitness.com/tennis-monitoring-sheet/

2. **External distractions.** By external distractions, I mean the opposite sex, computer games, spending time with friends, other sports and discovering other interests. It is important too, that you realise things will change from time to time; as young players develop, so too their interests and desires. More often than not, the more you try and restrict certain things, the more they may rebel or be inclined to lose interest in the things they have been focused on for years. Keeping young players balanced is the key here; if they are socially interacting away from tennis, are involved in other sports and have free time to do other things they enjoy, they will be less inclined to lose motivation for tennis and drift away. Allowing them to be young adults is important for them and their tennis development.

3. **Communication.** Asking questions like: "What are you enjoying about your lessons/training?", "What do you enjoy about tennis?", and "What do you feel we need to change to make things better?" allow you to have an open line of communication with young players and get them thinking about their tennis, not just doing it.

4. **External negativity.** Parents, coaches, trainers, friends and relatives that display impatience, aggressive behavior or dismissive body language towards young players, will have a detrimental effect on their attitude and motivation. These negative behaviors can ruin a young player's confidence and self-belief.

3. The Young Tennis Player

3.1 5 Essential attributes every young tennis player needs

1. **Attitude** – By far this is the number one attribute young players should strive to achieve and maintain. Having a positive, competitive, hard working attitude will put any young player in good stead. A healthy attitude will not only benefit a young player's tennis game, it will draw the attention of coaches and other players, who will respect them and you will find more people willing to help out if needed.

2. **Persistence** – Being persistent means, waking up every morning and following a plan, following it with passion, day in day, day out, no matter what the weather is like or how they are feeling, giving 100% in that moment. That's how progress comes.

3. **Discipline** – Young players need to learn how to control what they can control; discipline gives them more control over more things. Control will improve their game and other aspects of their lives. Discipline, in many areas, is needed to get the most out of a young player; including: diet, recovery, hydration, off court training, punctuality, court conduct and respect for others.

4. **Focus** – When young players show up to practice, they need to be ready and focused for the entire session; this is how they develop vital match play skills. It is too easy to show up and go through the motions; any young player can do that.

Striving to remain focused, and in the moment, will set up a valuable skill set for the future.

5. **Hard work ethic** – Any player who has made it to the top has worked hard, day in, day out for years and years. That is a given. Young players, who want to maximise their potential, need to do exactly the same. Hard work ethic is about putting in 100% effort, 100% intensity in every session. Chasing balls, never giving up and staying committed is expected every time. Sometimes parents tend to be too soft on their children, especially in western societies. Don't be afraid to encourage young players to push themselves, otherwise they will never know how much they have and what their limits are.

3.2 Important physical changes you need to be aware of

As young players develop, there are numerous changes occurring in their bodies. It is important to understand the changes occurring and what you need to watch out for, in order to prevent injuries.

We can break the developmental stages of young players into two categories; Childhood and Adolescence. Below, you will find information on certain growth stages and what you can expect to see happening.

Childhood – From ages 8-13 years

- Steady growth rate, 2-3 inches (5-8 cm) per year
- Brain growth, advanced motor function (running, jumping, catching etc.)
- Muscle development, increased strength and coordination. Movements should become smoother, stronger and more co-ordinated.
- Fine motor skills, increase in control of fingers etc.
- Children begin to lose their baby fat
- Children tend to talk a lot as their conversational skills develop. They may ask more questions regarding their tennis program etc.
- Children will become more individual, may express their opinions and want needs met.
- Children will have to deal with social pressures as they try to "fit in"
- They will begin to bond with certain individuals, identifying them as close friends. It is important to make sure they are spending time with the right people and children.

Adolescence - From ages 13-18 years

- Greatest amount of growth in height and weight.
- Growth spurts (fast growth periods)
- Puberty (sexual maturation)
- Brain development. Improved self-control, skills in planning, problem solving and decision-making.
- Due to fast growth, the centre of gravity changes and it can take time for young players to adjust. During fast growth periods, players may seem clumsy and their balance and co-ordination may seem impaired.
- Muscle strength and size will increase.
- Joints can be vulnerable. Bones can grow rapidly and muscle, tendon and ligaments my not have developed enough to fully support the localised joint.
- Each young player will physically develop at his or her own growth rate; a lot of this comes down to their genetics. Some players will have large growth spurts for 2 years while others may have smaller ones for 4 years.

Conditions and injuries you may come across when dealing with young players may include: knee pain, shoulder pain, ankle pain, wrist pain, back pain, swelling around joints, blisters, excessive sweating and stomach upsets. Common sense rules apply in regard to monitoring a young player's physical development and injuries. If they feel, or show any signs of pain or discomfort, especially for prolonged periods of time, they must be assessed by a qualified professional (physiotherapist, doctor etc.). It is a good idea to use what we call the 1-10 pain scale (1 being very slight pain, 10 being total agony) as this is the best way to monitor injuries. The more you use it, the better the young player will get at reading their pain. A young player should not take part in any activity that causes them to be in pain over 3 out of 10;

you will be putting them at risk. At the earliest sign of an injury, seek guidance on how to best deal with it.

1-10 Pain scale graph

1. Slight pain, can continue.

2. Slight pain, can continue.

3. Slight pain, can continue.

4. Train with caution, reduce training load or train other body parts.

5. Train with caution, reduce training load or train other body parts.

6-10. Cease training/matches. Seek professional medical attention (physiotherapist, sports doctor etc).

In some cases, players maybe able to continue training/ playing if the injury can be contained (strapped/ immobilised) and the chances of the injury worsening are very minimal. It is important to note in most instances some form of training can be performed. Working around or away for the injury site e.g. if you were to have a wrist injury, you could still train your lower body. Injuries that reach a 6 and above out of 10 should always be fully rehabilitated to ensure that injury should not become chronic and long term. The best thing your can do for the young player in this circumstance, is seek professional medical advice.

3.3 Benefits of playing tennis

Below is a list of some of the benefits that are associated with regular tennis practice, matches and off court tennis training.

1. **Improved aerobic and cardiovascular fitness** – helps with endurance and maintaining energy levels.

2. **Anaerobic fitness** – helps with high intensity training and recovery during exercise.

3. **Speed** – Young players are constantly chasing down balls and challenging their fast twitch muscle fibres. This leads to an increase in overall speed.

4. **Explosive power** – Jumping in multiple directions, driving forward and hitting with speed are all explosive movements that challenge the body in many ways. Young players, who are exposed to these movements and forces regularly, will develop more body control through the movements, giving them an increase in power.

5. **Flexibility** – Exercise is one of the best ways to increase a young player's flexibility.

6. **Strength** – One of the most important benefits of tennis is the strength gain associated with it. Through regular playing and training, young players will develop strength throughout their whole body. This will not only help their tennis and other sporting activities, it will make them less susceptible to not only sporting injuries, but also to everyday injuries.

7. **Co ordination** – There are various co ordination combinations involved with tennis. Hand to eye and foot to eye coordination are challenged extensively through tennis practice and match play. This leads to an increase in response, physical control and timing.

8. **Gross motor control** – Regular tennis will give young players the ability to have more control

over their large muscle groups. This means they will move quicker and gain more power and strength. This is important for injury prevention.

9. **Fine motor control** – Tennis is not only about hitting the ball as hard as you can. Young players need to learn how to be delicate, control certain shots and create angles. These fine motor skills are helpful for many aspects of life.

10. **Agility** – Due to the multi directional nature of tennis, young players will develop an increase in the ability to start/stop and change direction.

11. **Balance** – Tennis involves a lot of unilateral loading like landing on one leg and, hitting from one side at a time. These loading patterns require young players to develop balance through their whole body, in particular their lower extremities.

12. **Bone strength and bone density** – Exercise helps strengthen the bones of young players and, due to the dynamic nature of tennis; it also helps develop bone density.

13. **Commitment and work ethic** – When young players work hard consistently, they learn valuable lessons about themselves and how rewarding it can be.

14. **Discipline** – Tennis is a very complex and challenging sport. The better young players get, the more disciplined they must be; this will positively affect all aspects of their lives.

15. **Mistake and risk management** – Tennis gives young players the opportunity to learn about

playing within your abilities and realising that managing and minimising mistakes in tennis, or life, is critical.

16. **Responsibility for actions** – They soon learn that they are responsible for their actions on court; that they are alone. How they play, behave and deal with circumstances comes down to them. This teaches them a valuable life lesson; "Be responsible for what you do."

17. Ultimately it will give them the skills to make the right decision at the right time.

18. **Sportsmanship** – Tennis has rules and etiquette. Players are taught to play fair and accept the result, either win or lose. This helps when dealing with wins or losses throughout life.

19. **Learning to adapt** – Tennis is played on various surfaces and in different environmental settings. Things can change quickly during a match. Players learn to adapt and stay focused during these times.

20. **Problem solving** – Tennis offers a range of twists and turns from tweaking techniques to working out an opponent's serve. Players are constantly solving various issues throughout practice and matches. This skill has a good effect outside the court also, as they can use it to help solve everyday problems faster and with greater ease.

21. **Learn social skills** – Young players interact with others at practice and during tournaments. It is a great environment for them to realise that they can compete and still have a social connection.

4. Tennis Parents

4.1 Juggling schooling and full time tennis

Lleyton Hewitt was on the ATP tour at the age of 15, but let's face it; he was a very rare case. It is not often you hear of players pulling out of school at the age of 14 to chase life on the tour. If the young player you are dealing with has extraordinary potential and is already in a national system, with sponsors, and is looking to break through on the Pro tour soon, then you fall into a very small category. The best option for a player in this situation is distance education that is heavily monitored. For most young players out there, it can be a little more complicated working out the best plan.

It can be challenging to know the best way forward with a young player's tennis future. Should they play more tennis and do less schooling, or stay in school full time and work their tennis program as best they can. It is a challenge to get it right and it may take some time to find what is best for the young player.

Over the years we have seen many young players structure their tennis and schooling programs in different ways. Many of these players have chopped and changed until they have the balance and the program that works best for them; some have never got it right and have ended up pulling away from tennis. We recommend young players aged 15 years and under stay in a fulltime school program.

There are a few things to consider when deciding what to do with a young player's education/tennis plan.

- It is important to communicate with the young player and get their perspective, as well as the coaches, teachers and some close friends. Everyone will be able to offer different perspectives, which should make the decisions easier.

- Young players do not have the life experience to make big decisions; the parent/s is/are responsible for the final decision and the young player should not make it.

- You need to consider costing and the implications of the decision. Whatever your decision is; can you afford it?

- How will the young player be affected socially by the decision? Fulltime tennis can have different social settings and dynamics or interaction on a different level.

- How will the young player handle the pressure of fulltime tennis? Some young players may feel it is a burden because people have sacrificed (financially and time) for them and they may feel they cannot live up to it.

- We recommend you speak to as many older players as possible and get some feedback from them. There is a good chance they will be able to offer some good advice.

- Have an older player as a mentor. This is a great way for young players to learn and gather experience. They will gain valuable knowledge through having a mentor. A mentor will help guide them through decisions and give them feedback on various things.

- This last point is probably the most important; we are going to be totally honest and upfront with you. Young players should not throw the chance of an education away at a young age with the hope of making it on the tour. The statistics are frightfully low on players that make it to the top. If a young player has potential, works hard, has a low injury rate, has financial backing and some serious luck, they have a chance, BUT it is always great to have a good education to fall back on; maybe even give themselves an option to get a college tennis scholarship in another country.

Obviously there are many options regarding this topic, let's take a look at some.

- Full time tennis with no schooling (not recommended for young players under 18 years old)

- Full time tennis with distance education. This can be challenging, as young players need to be very disciplined. It is hard to study after training all day.

- Full time tennis with onsite education (usually in tennis academies worldwide)

- Full time schooling with after school tennis (this is what most young players do through to the age of 15-16 years of age)

- Full time schooling with a tennis program worked in at the school. Some schools offer sports programs for athletes. This is a good option for young players.

- Part time schooling. Some schools offer education programs for young players that allow them to finish their schooling over a longer period of time, allowing them to take more time away from school to focus on their tennis. This can be challenging as young players may lose focus and motivation for schooling as it can feel like it is dragging out.

In our opinion the best scenario is full time schooling until at least 16 years old, in a school that encourages and supports an individual's sporting endeavours. The young players will have the support they need whilst adjustments can be made to assist with their schooling requirements. Most schools worldwide will cater for the needs of young athletes, as long as the system is not abused and the young player does what is required academically. A good option is to ask around and try to find a school that has a focus on tennis; they will generally have a solid tennis program in place that works well within the school environment. We recommend young players have short stints overseas during their school holidays or if time off can be arranged with their school. 4-8 week blocks work well, starting out at the age of 14 years, with a parent or guardian to accompany them. We have found this works very well, as young players get exposed to other tennis dynamics, intensities and systems. It also gives them the chance to learn from other cultures and get some life experience. It shows them firsthand how hard you will need to work if you want to make it. There are a lot of world-class tennis academies around, but it is always good to go where you have been recommended, so ask around and check online.

4.2 Financial costs involved in building a champion

The costs involved in building a champion, can be high. Here are some key factors to consider and budget for. Obviously, the final cost will depend on the amount of tennis practised, played and off-court work.

- Coaching: Group squad training $15-$30 per hour. One on one coaching: $60-$150 per hour.
- Tennis specific fitness training: $70-$120 per hour.
- Equipment:
  a. Racquets x 1-3 $80-$300
  b. Stringing $20-$100 per month
  c. Grips and misc. $15-$50 per month
- Clothing: shoes, socks, match/practice clothes, hats etc. $40-$250 per month.
- Tournament fees: $50-$150 per tournament.
- Travel to tournaments: petrol, flights, train fares etc.
- Food and fluids. Due to exercise demands, appetite increases, which equals more food and fluids consumed.

It is really important to have a monthly budget and work with it as best you can. Prioritise according to the goals. There are lots of ways to save money: pairing up and sharing the costs for tennis/fitness lessons, looking for sponsors for equipment, shopping around for equipment and clothing (online), not worrying about big brands (wear what is comfortable and appropriate), car pooling to practice and tournaments, taking meals, snacks and drinks with you, rather than constantly buying them when you are out.

4.3 Keeping young players socially active

Tennis can be a very individual and isolated sport, if you let it! Keeping young players socially active will help keep them balanced, allow them to channel their emotions and develop social interaction skills. Encourage them to make friends with their peers. Even though tennis is an individual sport, it is always played in a social setting and that is why the vast majority of people play the game. Knowing when to play for fun and when to be serious is important. Young players should be able to play against their peers and be friends off court. Organising BBQ's after

matches or tournaments is one way of getting young players to spend time with friends, away from tennis. Their friends don't always have to be tennis friends; in fact, getting them socially active away from tennis, is a great way to clear their "tennis head", keeping them fresh for the tennis environment.

It is important to not over inflate their ego. Keep it real and in check. A young player may have potential to be a star one-day, and they may be one of the best in their circle, but as they develop and change circles, their position changes too. If you keep inflating their ego, they will have problems with other players in development squads and school based teams, which could tarnish and jeopardise their enjoyment. Keeping them involved in other sports is a good way to get them interacting with other children; team sports give them the opportunity to socially interact in a different environment and can develop a good sense of teamwork and appreciation of others.

4.4 Tips for parents on reaching the top

1. **Be committed**

   Tennis is a complicated and complex sport, which is why we love being a part of it. There is a lot involved, so getting things right is important. If you want your young player/s to reach the top, you need to do all you can to make it happen. Don't rely on things just happening, make things happen, be pro active and learn as much as you can from people who know.

2. **Get the balance right**

   Find what works best for each young player and stick with it. Give them routine, consistency and support. Then, they will thrive.

3. **Your number one goal, BE SUPPORTIVE**

Watch, listen and give advice in a supportive way at the right time. Remember, everyone has their place and their role to play. What is your role? How effectively are you going to carry it out?

4. **Be patient**

It takes time for young players to develop the skills, co ordination, strength and conditioning to become a top player. Don't put too much pressure on them. As long as they are consistent, making progress and enjoying the process, it will all come together. If you follow all the advice in this book they should have the motivation, dedication and belief to reach their potential.

5. **Communicate with the team**

It will be very hard to make it on your own. Coaching, managing, training and scheduling young players is not a one-person job. It can take 30 years to get proficient enough in all those areas to make it work. Find your team and have a strong, open line of communication with them all. Don't wait until things become a big issue; make time to discuss things and nip it in the bud. Young players get very disheartened and unmotivated when they are continually changing coaches, trainers etc. Believe in the team, but at the same time be willing to question things at the right time, if you feel it is needed.

4.5 From the coach – 14 things to know

1. Let the coach/trainer do their job. It is very rare that a coach/trainer tells a parent how to be a parent, so a parent should not tell a coach or trainer how to coach. Let the coach/trainer do what you are paying them for. Have faith in the team you have chosen, or find a new one, that you have faith in. If you need to discuss coaching/ training matters, arrange a time with the coach/ trainer and explain your matters then.

2. When speaking with a coach/trainer with the young player present, don't speak negatively or aggressively about the player. This will lead to the young player feeling uncomfortable and embarrassed and can lead to a lack of motivation and interest for the game. It is best to plan a time to discuss things with a coach/trainer via phone or face to face. Together, you can come up with a plan to resolve any issues.

3. You need to invest many hours travelling them around. Practice, matches, training etc., it all adds up. Be prepared to get behind the driving wheel. A tip for this area is to make the time waiting around for practice to finish etc. useful for yourself; watch your child for a few minutes, then head off for a walk, run or tennis lesson yourself. Reading and doing some work will be beneficial too. We have a client whose father brings him in; the father is working as he walks in the door, blue tooth headset on, computer on, typing away. He will sit and work until the session is done, ask a few questions at the end, book the next session and he is off. Great stuff!

4. It's a financial commitment, be prepared. It is scary to think how much money gets invested over years, getting a young player to maximise their ability. Any sport has its expenses, so be prepared and have a plan in place, know what you are spending and where. The coaching and training is necessary, the fancy clothes and over spending on equipment and gear, not so much. Have a budget for coaching/training and also for clothing and equipment.

5. It's not about you. You might be sitting there thinking, "How rude! It's not about me at all"; most parents think that and hopefully for you, you are right. If you are trying to live your dream through your child, the wheels will fall off. As a parent, it is your responsibility to do what is right for your child, to have their best interests at the forefront of your actions.

6. Young players need your interest and support, but not all the time. Give them the freedom to play without you there too. Don't hang around all the time, analysing everything they do or making comments; that drives a coach bonkers. It is best to keep your mouth closed during practice sessions and find the right time to discuss issues.

7. Be very careful not to over inflate their ego. Telling them, all the time, how good they are, and that they are the best, will lead to big drops in confidence when they realise they are not. It is best to talk about their improvements and how much progress they have made; they will draw enough confidence out of that.

8. Be flexible. They are growing, they are changing. Some weeks/months, they won't want to play tennis or continue with the schedule and that's ok. During these times, you and all of the team need to be flexible and compromise, without giving in. Look to change things up, if needed. Your child will respond and return to tennis hungrier, if you manage these times effectively.

9. Balance and Education. It is critical that you keep a healthy balance of tennis, education and down time in your child's life. Education is more important than anything else they will ever do in life. Without a solid education, they will limit their potential later in life. It is important that your child still gets to socialise away from tennis. When tennis consumes their life, this is when they lose interest and walk away.

10. Learn how to talk to your child before and after a match or session. Get advice from the coach on this.

11. Learn how to behave on the side of a court. We call this "Tennis spectator etiquette". It is one of the most important things to learn to do well. Your body language, comments and attitude will dramatically affect your child's performance, not only for the particular match, but also for the future. Never comment aggressively or negatively about the child's opponent, never use abusive language toward your child or their opponent, keep your body language positive, by sitting or standing with confidence, don't shake your head or wave your arms around at them. Use comments like: "Keep it going", "You're doing

well", "Keep trying", "Good work", "That's the way", "C'mon, you can do this". Remember, you are there to support them.

12. Be organised. Learn how to manage all the weekly activities by keeping a diary. If you have a few kids who play sport or out of school activities, you know how hard it can be getting everyone where they should be, on time. Think ahead and be prepared. Have snacks, clothes, forms etc. ready to go; better still, we encourage parents to get their children to organise their snacks, clothes etc. with adult supervision, and to communicate what is going on the next day so they know things like: when they are getting picked up, what they are doing, what they need to have ready etc. Make them accountable and responsible as well. It will help you in the short term and them in the long term, Win–Win!!!

13. Focus more on improvement than results. This is a simple point that should not be complicated. Focus more on their progress, rather than their match results.

5. Court Etiquette

5.1 How should a young player act on court?

A young player's conduct during tournaments really should not differ that much from their day-to-day training. A good attitude is developed on the practice court and carried to the match court. You do need to be respectful of your opponent but also be competing at 100%. The best example I can think of is Nadal. He always gives it his all with a sportsman-like manner, no matter whom he is playing. If he does happen to lose, he never has any excuses. It is the coach's job to educate young players on correct conduct; parents should support their approach and reinforce it.

It can take time to develop emotional control for young players; it is a good idea to start teaching players, at a young age that they are responsible for how they act, their actions and the outcomes. If a match does not go their way, they need to learn how to control the situation and how they react to it. This is where a sport psychologist comes in. We have seen a lot of young players benefit from a few consultations with a sports psychologist. They will learn some simple strategies depending on their issues. The most issues are: staying focused, keeping their cool and dealing with defeat

6. Training Programs

6.1 Off court sport – combining tennis with other activities

Young tennis players should play other sports. Playing other sports actually has a lot of benefits for their tennis skills and tennis fitness. Some of those benefits include:

1. Co-ordination
2. Endurance
3. Reaction
4. Agility and Speed
5. Strength
6. Stability
7. Flexibility
8. Injury prevention

Complementary sports that will help improve speed, agility, co ordination, endurance and social awareness are: soccer, basketball, netball, squash and athletics.

Complementary sports that will help improve strength, stability, flexibility and injury prevention include: gymnastics, swimming and dancing.

Team sports will allow young players to become more balanced and socially aware. Team sports also give them the opportunity to see how other children respond and perform in competitive situations. They will pick up some valuable experience about competing, fair play and working hard.

Through the ages of 5-10, it is important for children to play multiple sports. As a guide, these sports could include; tennis x 2-3 weekly, soccer/netball/gymnastics/dancing x 1-2 weekly and swimming x 1 weekly.

Through the ages of 11-14, it is important for children to play a few sports, with a large focus on tennis. As a guide, these sports could include; tennis x 3-4 weekly, soccer/netball/athletics x 1-2 weekly and swimming x 1 weekly.

Through the ages of 15-18, it is important for children to play one other sport to complement tennis. This sport could be: soccer, netball, squash or basketball, played once or twice a week. Swimming should also be continued, as a form of recovery and muscle endurance, at least once a week, particularly at the end of the week.

It is important to get the balance right through all levels of development. Most parents will tend to overdo it with their children and get them playing and training too much. Generally, children who excel at tennis, have the potential to do well in other sports as well. To make it to the top, tennis requires a lot of time on court and commitment also off the court. From the age of 14 onward, it is important to have a strong focus on tennis and consider other sports as secondary and a chance to unwind from tennis, keep active and fine-tune skills: hand-eye co ordination, foot-eye co ordination, competing, that ultimately will help improve the tennis game.

6.2 Benefits of Tennis Fitness Training

Tennis Fitness Benefits

Tennis fitness training has many benefits, it can positively impact a young players tennis game, not only in the short term, but also more importantly in the long term. If you want young players to remain injury free, have the energy, strength and power needed to maximise their potential, then finding the right tennis specific trainer and tennis fitness program is your first step.

Here are some of the benefits that tennis fitness training will have on a young players game.

Strength and Power training will:

- Help young players get more out of their serve and shots from the first point until the last point.
- Give young players the ability to transfer power through their legs and core, giving them more power through all their shots.
- Build a good strength foundation that will lead to power development throughout the body.
- Recruit fast twitch fibres in the muscle, making young players more dynamic on court and dramatically increase power in their forehand, backhand and serve.

Agility, Footwork and Speed training will:

- Help improve quickness, reaction and foot speed on court.
- Reduce the chances of being wrong footed by their opponent.
- Give them the confidence to run down every ball.
- Make them feel lighter, have a more explosive first step and become more efficient on court.
- Help young players decelerate more efficiently into each shot.
- Give young players more time in preparing for a shot, which helps improve their decision making, this dramatically increases control in their shots and allows them to play better percentage tennis.
- Increase the ability to accelerate out of their shot, back into position for their next shot.

Core /Injury Prevention Exercises will:

- Give young players more balance and stability throughout their body, which enables them to have more control on each shot.

- Encourage a young player to stay low, and keeps them strong over the ball.

- Help young players stand their ground and not get pushed back off the ball or off the back off the court.

- Help eliminate career-ending injuries. Injuries can often be prevented, with regular core and stability exercises.

- Give young players the chance to play more tournaments. Missing important tournaments through injury can be frustrating; a strong core will help keep players on court longer.

- Help manage and prevent old injuries reoccurring.

Tennis specific Stretching/Foam rolling exercises will

- Help reduce soreness and fatigue from day to day training or a hard match.

- Give players the capacity to back up the next day feeling fresh and revitalized and ready to give it 100% again.

- Lengthen muscles and help to increase circulation to recovering muscle groups, giving young players a faster recovery.

- Enhance equilibrium and muscle balance throughout the body.

- Free up joints and muscles, which increase range of movement. This is the best way to get more out of your shots whilst preventing any injuries.

Tennis specific Warm up exercises will

- Prepare a young players body for tennis. By raising body temperature, it increases blood flow, which increases circulation of oxygen and nutrients around the body.

- Ensure young players are ready to go from the first ball; they will be on their toes! more reactive and mentally switched on.

- Loosen tight muscles and activate weak muscles (through recruitment warm up exercises) this allows young players to get as much as 20% more out of their practice or match.

For more information on Tennis Fitness Programs please visit http://tennisfitness. com/online-tennis-programs/

6.3 How much a young tennis player needs to practice/play or train for tennis?

In order to improve your tennis performance, it is important to physically work hard, but it is just as important to rest and recover hard! Vigorous, prolonged tennis exercise breaks down muscle tissue, fatigues the nervous system and overall places the body under stress. It is during the rest and recovery period that the body gets the positive physical and emotional gains; among them cardio vascular and physical and mental strength.

If there is an overload of volume (amount of tennis training) and intensity (level of energy used) with inadequate recovery time between sessions, a player will start to develop physical, behavioral and emotional issues. This scenario can be classified as a condition called **Overtraining**. Overtraining, or burnout, is a common problem for many athletes of all ages in many sports. It is often seen in young tennis players, possibly due to the fact that they find it harder to communicate how they are feeling and are not as in tune with their bodies as adults.

Symptoms of over training for tennis can include: persistent muscle soreness, persistent fatigue, elevated resting heart rate, increased susceptibility to infections, increased incidence of injuries, irritability, mental breakdown, loss of appetite, mood swings, loss of motivation, loss of enthusiasm, loss of competitive drive, burn out and abandonment of the sport.

For these reasons, associations like the WTA have applied age restrictions that don't allow players to turn professional until they reach a certain age. Many international federations monitor and plan the junior players' calendar to avoid burnout.

How long, intense and often a player practices, trains and plays tournaments is very much an individual thing. We are all built slightly differently and need to be treated differently. There is no generic perfect ratio; it is what works best for each individual, young or old. What is important is to work out the right balance for each tennis player, and ensure they have **one full day rest per week**. Quality over quantity should always be the goal.

Below is only a guideline for a tennis player's workload:

Age	Tennis	Fitness or Other sports	Total
6-8yrs	2-3 days 45mins	2-3 days 45mins	3 - 4.5hrs
9-11yrs	3-4 days 1hr	2-3 days 1hr	5 - 7hrs
12-14yrs	4-5 days 1-2hrs	3-4 days 1hr	7 - 14hrs
15-16yrs	4-5 days 2-3hrs	3-4 days 1hr	11 - 19hrs
16-18yrs	5-6 days 3-4hrs	3-5 days 1hr	18 - 29hrs

6.4 Ideal training week for different ages

6-8yrs old (Between 3 - 4.5hrs per week)								
	Mon	Tues	Wed	Thurs	Fri	Sat	Sun	Total
Tennis	45mins		45mins		45mins		Rest	2.25hrs
Fitness/ Other Sports		45mins		45mins		45mins	Rest	2.25hrs

9-11yrs old (Between 5-7hrs per week)								
	Mon	Tues	Wed	Thurs	Frid	Sat	Sun	Total
Tennis	1hr	1hr		1hr	1hr		Rest	4hrs
Fitness/ Other Sports	1hr		1hr			1hr	Rest	3hrs

12-14yrs old (Between 7-14hrs per week)								
	Mon	Tues	Wed	Thurs	Frid	Sat	Sun	Total
Tennis	1-2hrs	1-2hrs		1-2hrs	1-2hrs	1-2hrs	Rest	10hrs
Fitness/ Other Sports	1hr		1hr	1hr	1hr		Rest	4hrs

15-16yrs old (Between 11-19hrs per week)							
	Mon	Tues	Wed	Thurs	Frid	Sat	Sun	Total
Tennis	2-3hrs	2-3hrs		2-3hrs	2-3hrs	2-3hrs	Rest	15hrs
Fitness	1hr		1hr	1hr	1hr		Rest	4hrs

16-18yrs old (Between 19-29hrs per week)							
	Mon	Tues	Wed	Thurs	Frid	Sat	Sun	Total
Tennis	3-4hrs	3-4hrs	3-4hrs	3-4hrs	3-4hrs	3-4hrs	Rest	24hrs
Fitness	1hr	1hr	1hr	1hr	1hr		Rest	5hrs

To find the right balance for each player, we recommend, each quarter, monitoring how a player is feeling on a daily basis. Write down how they feel each day for one month. Areas to be included are: energy levels, sleep quality, nutrition/hydration and motivation. You can use a scale of 1 to 5 (5: feeling extremely fatigued and sore and 1: feeling fresh and full of energy). Once you have the records, you can go back and compare the results to the volume and intensity of certain periods of the month. Look to make changes to keep the athlete consistently around a 1-3 on the scale.

Whether you are a coach, player or parent of a tennis player, it is important to get the balance right. Seek advice from qualified professionals: coaches and tennis fitness trainers, and always make sure the player/s have had some form of involvement in the process of determining how long, how often and how intense their tennis training is.

6.5 How important is it to warm up?

If you want young players to get the most out of their tennis practices, perform well in matches and prevent injuries, then having a consistent, tennis specific warm up plan is essential. In all reality, it should take a young player 10min to warm up; it's not a great deal of time and the benefits are huge. They will be more physically reactive and mentally, more responsive. Below is a list of benefits associated with an adequate tennis warm up:

1. Increases blood flow to muscle.

2. Helps to lengthen out muscle, preparing it for exercise.

3. Stimulates the nervous system

Working with young players for many years, we have found some common things happen regarding warming up:

1. Some young players get to training on time, or even early, but sit around until instructed to warm up.

2. Some young players are consistently late for training and don't warm up at all, or have a short ineffective warm up.

3. Their warm up is not performed with enough effort and intensity.

In the 3 examples above, the coach or trainer will need to spend 10min to warm the young player up. That is 10min out of their session, 10min that could be used doing something more productive.

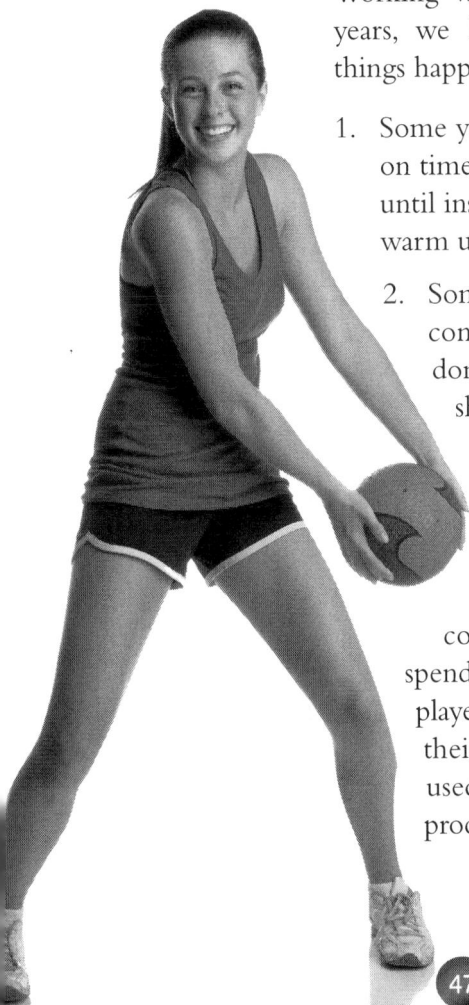

Although it is partly the role of the coach/fitness trainer to get the young player motivated for sessions, it is equally the responsibility of the player to get the warm up done prior to their session.

This is how it should work.

1. The young player is given their warm up program from their coach or preferably from a tennis specific trainer.

2. The young player gets to training 10min before their session starts and performs the warm up; 15min if they want to chat with friends before they start.

3. After the warm up, players should feel "Ready to go" not half ready to go.

You can imagine how much more a young player will get out of their sessions if they are ready from the onset. They will be more alert, reactive and responsive. They can get up to **20% more out of a session**. In the long term that plays a big factor in progression and results.

Please note. Children can feel embarrassed if they show up late for training, especially if it is in a squad and if it happens regularly; they may get unmotivated to attend. If your child gets to training late regularly, you need to establish who is responsible for that and address the situation. Sometimes, external influences occur (traffic etc.) or training times just do not suit and you may need to find a more effective time. There are also instances where parent's lateness affects the situation; it is important to find the problem and address it.

(For information on how to warm up go to our website www.tennisfitness.com; you can purchase specific tennis warm up programs) http://tennisfitness.com/warm-up-programs/

6.6 How important is it to stretch?

Stretching plays an important role in a young player's development and results, not only short term, but also long term. Let's quickly look at what stretching is and what it does.

Stretching is a form of physical exercise in which a specific muscle, tendon, or muscle group, is deliberately flexed or stretched in order to improve the muscle's elasticity and achieve comfortable muscle tone. The result is a feeling of increased muscle control, flexibility and range of motion.

Types of stretching

1. **Ballistic** – Getting to the end range of a stretch and lightly moving or gently bouncing, with control.

2. **PNF** – Getting to the end range of a stretch and pushing back against someone or something for a short period of time.

3. **Static** – Getting to the end range of a stretch and holding the stretch for a set length of time. Static stretching isolates targeted muscle groups.

4. **Dynamic** – movement based stretching; an example of this would be squatting up and down for a set time.

It is common for athletes to stretch before but mainly after exercise in order to reduce injury and increase performance. Stretching helps improve flexibility, which enables more fluid movement and a greater range of motion. It helps blood circulation to the muscle; the more blood flow, the more chance of a quicker recovery. Stretching assists in joint function, especially dynamic stretching; lengthening the muscle out around a joint will help it move and function better, reducing the risk of injury.

We encourage all players to incorporate stretching plans into their tennis programs.

This is what we recommend:

Pre tennis/fitness (once warmed up)

1. Dynamic stretching, using up to 6 tennis specific movement based stretches.

2. Static stretching, only if a certain muscle feels particularly tight.

Post tennis/fitness (within 2 hours)

1. Static stretching; for young players 4-6 stretches to start will be enough, otherwise they tend to get bored and it seems like a chore.

2. PNF – to release a specific area of tension e.g. hamstrings once to twice a week.

We highly recommend a stretching plan pre (dynamic) and post training (static). In fact, we consider it a necessity if you want to reach the top.

(For more information on tennis specific stretches, visit our website www. tennisfitness.com. You are able to purchase our tennis specific stretching program) http://tennisfitness.com/stretching-programs/

7. Tennis Nutrition

Before we look at what young players should be eating to get the most out of themselves, there are some key points we want to make:

1. **Education** – All children are individual and they have varying tastes and food likes and dislikes. If your child does not like eating certain foods, it is still important to encourage them to eat it and explain, as best you can, the reasons why. Their tastes and food likes are likely to change as they develop and continue to grow; if they have been exposed to various healthy foods at a young age, they will be more inclined to try things as they get older. Food is fuel, if you want young players to perform and feel good, they need to fuel their bodies with the correct foods.

2. **Be an example** –If your child sees you eating foods that you encourage them to eat, they will be more likely to eat those foods as well.

3. **Preparation** – Have snacks and meals planned as best you can; write out a list of snacks and meals weekly. Have snacks ready to go all the time, leaving them stored in the fridge or pantry.

4. **Routine** – Once you establish a healthy eating plan for your child, it is important to maintain it. This is where the planning and preparation will help. Your child will have their favourite snacks and meals; aim to work with these as best you can, but make sure you regularly mix meals and snacks up. Give them variety using the healthy foods they enjoy.

5. **Work with your child** – Ask for feedback on the food they are eating. They will be more inclined to eat their snacks and meals if they involved in the selection process.

7.1 Foods

Carbohydrates, Fats and Protein - what are they and what do they do? Before we look at what young players should eat, let's break food down and see what certain foods actually do.

Carbohydrates

Carbohydrates are the best fuel source for athletes because they provide the glucose used for energy and brain function. Glucose is stored as glycogen in the muscles and liver. Muscle glycogen is the most readily available energy source for working muscle and can be released more quickly than other energy sources. Carbohydrates should comprise 45% to 65% of total caloric intake for 4 to 18 year olds. Good sources of carbohydrates include: whole grains, pasta, rice, vegetables and fruits.

Protein

Protein builds and repairs muscle. For mild exercise and exercise of short duration, proteins do not act as a primary source of energy. Protein should comprise approximately 10% to 30% of total energy intake for 4 to 18 year olds. Good sources of protein include: lean meat and poultry, fish, eggs, dairy products, beans and nuts.

Fats

Fat provides energy, insulation and protects vital organs. Fats should comprise approximately 25% to 35% of total energy intake for 4 to 18 year olds. Good sources of fat include: lean meat and poultry, fish, nuts, seeds, dairy products, avocado, unsaturated oils. Saturated fats should comprise no more than 10% of total energy intake. Saturated fat from chips, candy, fried foods and baked goods should be minimised or totally restricted.

Simple nutrition is important for a young player's growth, achieving good health and providing energy. Sports nutrition enhances athletic performance by decreasing fatigue and the risk of injury or illness. One of the best factors about good nutrition is that it enables athletes to optimise their training and recovery. Balancing energy intake with energy expenditure is crucial to prevent an energy deficit or excess. Energy deficits can cause loss of muscle mass and increased susceptibility to fatigue, injury or illness. Energy excess can result in weight gain and obesity.

Energy requirements for adolescents are more variable, depending on age, activity level, growth rate and stage of physical maturity. Extra calories are needed during growth spurts and to replenish energy expended during physical activity. Seek advice from a professional Dietitian or Nutritionist to work out your daily calorie intake.

Here is an example of a 2500-calorie eating plan

Breakfast	Snack	Lunch	Snack	Dinner
Porridge with fruit 1 cup rolled oats, cooked 10 almonds 1 cup blueberries 30g raisins 1 cup full cream milk 1 cup of orange juice	Wholegrain snack bar (muesli bar) 1 medium pear	Ham and salad wrap, apple 1 large whole meal wrap, 100g sliced ham, 1/2 cup shredded lettuce, 1 small sliced tomato and 2 slices of beetroot, 1 tsp. of mayonnaise 1 medium apple	2 slices of cheddar cheese, 10 rice crackers.	Beef & vegetable stir-fry with rice, yoghurt 200gm beef, 1/2 cup carrots, 1/2 cup zucchini, 1/2 cup of broccoli, 1/4 cup onion, 1 tbsp. olive oil, 1 cup of cooked rice (brown or white) 200g of full cream flavoured yoghurt.
= 665 calories	= 228 calories	= 447 calories	= 211 calories	= 920 calories

Please Note - These are all general guidelines we suggest seeing a professional to calculate your child's energy requirements

Foods to avoid/foods to eat

Foods to avoid: fried foods (hot chips, schnitzel, donuts) and foods high in sugar (chocolate, candy, cakes, biscuits, soft drinks, ice cream)

Foods to eat moderately: Sauces, cheeses and unsaturated fats and oils.

Foods to eat: All fresh fruit and vegetables, whole grains such as brown and white rice, oats, pasta, sourdough or whole meal bread, fish, poultry − chicken and eggs, meat including beef, pork and veal, all nuts, dairy foods including yoghurt and milk.

7.2 What to eat before, during and after training/matches?

Before training, or a match, it is important to build up your energy stores; muscle glycogen.

Ideally, aim to eat 1.5-2.5 hours before a match / training. Carbohydrate rich foods are best; rice, pasta or whole meal bread. Avoid rich, heavy or fatty foods such as: deep fried meals, hot chips or rich pasta creamy sauces. Examples of foods to eat pre match or training are on page 60.

Stick with foods the young player is familiar with and that they enjoy to eat. The pre match/training main guidelines are: eat carbohydrate rich foods, low in protein, and low in fibre, nothing too heavy/fatty foods. Some players find it hard to eat anything before a match. That is one of the reasons why it is important to eat something sustainable 3 hours before play. They will be more inclined to eat more and have something there to use for fuel. If a young player really finds it hard to eat on match day, you should encourage them to eat in small amounts, every 30-45min; a piece of fruit, bite of a sandwich etc.

Post-match nutrition

After your match (or practice), your post-match nutrition becomes crucial for recovering your energy depletion. The first goal is to rehydrate, refuel, repair and revitalise.

Glycogen stores can take 24-48 hours to refill; it is important to start replenishing carbohydrates immediately following exercise, to accelerate the recovery process.

However, there may be very little appetite or opportunity to eat following a match. Drinking a liquid carbohydrate may be easier to consume and allows for glycogen replacement, restores lost electrolytes, and also promotes hydration.

In addition, it is equally important to drink water, since it takes three grams of water to store one gram of glycogen. Post-match protein intake in an easy to digest form, like a protein milk product or smoothie, may be an ideal way to help your muscles to immediately start to rebuild.

Within the first 30 minutes after your match: eat a large snack or medium portion meal with 2 parts carbohydrates, 1 part protein (e.g. sports drink or natural juices, energy bar or pasta/rice, with lean meat, and a vegetable) because:

- This is when your muscles are most effective at storing glycogen
- Your body is still using energy and burning calories
- Your cells are rehydrating

Within 2-3 hours after your match: eat a well-balanced meal including a variety of carbohydrate sources, a protein portion, and plenty of fluids because:

- Your body is still low on fluids, minerals, and energy
- What you eat at this time will restore most of the energy used during play
- Your muscles begin repairing any damage that may have occurred in the match
- A pasta/rice based meal with lean meat and vegetables with several glasses of fluid make an ideal post-match meal.

Within 24 hours after your match: continue to drink plenty of fluids and give your body a rest (if possible) because:

- It takes a while to fully recover from your match mentally and physically

- It often takes a while to fully replace the fluid you lost during a match.

- Your muscles need rest to store glycogen and repair themselves

If a player has another match scheduled to begin shortly after the completion of play (i.e. within 1-2 hrs), rehydration and carbohydrate intake should begin immediately.

High-carbohydrate sport drinks, sport bars, and other high-carbohydrate foods with a high GI, will facilitate the rapid restoration of muscle glycogen more so than other foods.

Finally, if sweat losses from the previous match were extensive, and especially if the player is prone to, or just experienced cramps, additional salt may be added to the diet. (This can be best prescribed by a qualified sports doctor or nutritionist).

Breakfast, lunch and dinner options

Breakfast	Lunch/Dinner	Snacks
2x poached eggs, avocado, tomato, spinach, sourdough x 2	Sandwiches: wholegrain, sourdough or rye bread with salad, turkey, chicken, tuna or ham.	Fruit salad
Porridge: Rolled Oats, Oatmeal/Millet/Quinoa, honey, stevia or cinnamon sprinkle, grated apple, grapes or blueberries with a sprinkle of LSA, coconut flakes, chai seeds	Grilled fish/prawn & salad	Smoothies (frozen berries, yoghurt, nuts, milk, coconut flesh & coconut water)
	BBQ chicken & salad	Yoghurt
	Vegetable stir fry, brown rice, chicken, lamb etc	Muesli, yoghurt, berries, cinnamon, honey
Omelette, spinach, ham, capsicum, tomato, onion etc.	Soups e.g. vegetable soup (no creamy sauces) + sourdough roll or rice cracker	Rice cakes, tuna, avocado/cottage/hummus, cheese, tomato
Boiled eggs, avocado, ham or turkey, sourdough x 2		Nuts
		Handful dried fruit
Scrambled eggs, avocado or hummus, tomato, ham or turkey, Sourdough x 2	Sushi Roll (brown rice) or sashimi	Fresh squeezed juice
Sliced apple, cinnamon yogurt, LSA, coconut flakes, chai seeds	Wraps – chicken, ham, turkey, lettuce, cheese, tomato, onion, capsicum etc.	Sourdough toast, honey, nut spread, cottage cheese
		Cracker with ham, turkey, hummus, cottage cheese
Oat meal pancakes, blueberries, apple, cinnamon		Sliced apples with tahini
Baked or poached apple/pear, crushed nuts, LSA, coconut flakes, chai seeds		Sliced banana with tahini and honey
		Sliced carrot, almond spread/hummus
Salmon avocado, tomato, sourdough x 2		Sliced celery, almond spread

To get our favourite Match Day Breakfast just contact us by clicking on this link http://tennisfitness.com/favourite-match-day-breakfast/

7.3 Hydration! What should a young player be drinking, how much and when?

When we talk about hydration, we are talking about any liquid that is consumed by someone: Water, soft drink, sports drinks, coffee, milk etc.

What should a young player be drinking?

We recommend water as the primary source of fluid to be consumed by young players. Water actually makes up more than half a person's body weight. It is relied on for many roles in the body; some of these include:

1. Helping distribute and carry nutrients, minerals and oxygen through the body.
2. Removal of waste products from the body (urine excretion).
3. Regulating body temperature through perspiration (sweating)
4. Lubricating joints.
5. Maintains blood volume.

Your body doesn't get water just from drinking water. Any fluid you drink will contain water, but water is the best choice. Most foods contain water, too. Fruit contains quite a bit of water, so to do vegetables.

Water is so important for the body; without it we would not be able to survive long (only days). Even after 1 day without consuming water, the body can start to have major problems. When "dehydration" (when the body does not have enough water in it to function properly) occurs, its effects can be life threatening.

Signs of dehydration that you need to look out for include:

Mild to moderate dehydration – Dry, sticky mouth, thirst, decreased urine output; urine may appear dark yellow in colour, dry skin, headache, dizziness or light-headedness.

Severe dehydration – Extreme thirst, extreme dizziness and a reduced rate of communication, lack of sweating, little or no urination, very dry mouth, rapid breathing, rapid heartbeat, unconsciousness.

If young players ever experience severe dehydration symptoms, it is essential they go straight to hospital and seek medical attention.

Even mild dehydration can have a big impact on a young player's performance. Lack of concentration, poor decision-making, and poor recovery can all be associated with dehydration.

Sports drinks

Sports drinks are designed to provide energy and replace electrolytes – sodium and potassium, which athletes lose in sweat. If a young player is going to be active for more than 45-60mins, sports drinks may be a good option. After exercising for 60 to 90 minutes, the body has probably used up its readily available sources of

energy and may benefit from a fluid that contains carbohydrates and electrolytes. Drinking water and a sports drink at this stage is good.

If your young athlete simply won't drink enough water, sports drinks are an option. Diluted fruit juice is another option; avoid carbonated beverages, soft drinks, during exercise as they can upset the stomach.

Why is this sports drink so good?

Coconut Water, dubbed "Mother Nature's Sports Drink" the life beverage, is all natural, low in carbs and sugar, 99% fat free and contains organic compounds, promoting health and wellness; helping to rehydrate and replenish fluids; a great sports replacement drink. It has more potassium than four bananas, and is super hydrating. It has fewer calories, less sodium, and more potassium than a sports drink. Great drink for post exercise if the player is water/flavor fatigued.

How much fluid should be consumed by young players and when?

Thirst is not always a reliable indicator of a young player's need for water. Make sure they drink plenty of water daily; before, during and after exercise. Studies indicate sweat rate may be as low as 300mL/hour or as high as 2.6L/hour (Sawaka et al 2007: ACSM Position Stand)

Visit http://www.powerade.com.au/Utilities/Hydration Calculator.html and follow the hydration calculator to learn how much water a child should drink each day. Remember these are just guides; you must keep an eye on how much young players are drinking and check for signs of dehydration, especially during hot, long days.

Hydration

Before training or a match. It is important to be hydrated. This can be achieved by drinking water regularly throughout the day. Every 20-30 min taking a few mouthfuls will help maintain hydration. The key to hydration is maintaining it. Staying hydrated all the time is the best way to prepare for any exercise.

Hydration tips

1. The simplest way to tell if a child is drinking enough is to check the colour and amount of urine excreted. If urine is pale, normal water balance has returned. If urine is dark, drink more water. If the urine output is minimal and an effort to pass, drink more water.

2. Ensure young players always have a full water bottle when they enter the court.

3. Be conscious of weather conditions. In hot or humid weather, young players will sweat more to help cool their body down, so more fluid will need to be consumed than at a milder temperature.

4. Educate young players on important hydration factors. Urine colour/output, dry mouth, thirst, drinking regularly and that water is the best option.

5. It will take a few months, but constantly reminding young players to drink water will eventually create a fantastic long-term habit.

During training or a match. Tennis is a game that gives players every opportunity to top up their energy stores and stay hydrated. During training sessions, coaches give players drink breaks and during matches, players get a chance to rest, snack and hydrate. Young players should utilise these breaks and they should start to get into the habit of getting it right from a young age. At every change of ends, players should hydrate, no matter the weather conditions or energy expenditure. Drinking water is best for the first 45min of play, after 45min they can introduce a sports drinks or coconut water. Sipping regularly is the best way to stay hydrated and avoids lots of toilet breaks. Some players prefer cold water/drinks during training or matches, this is a personal preference; however cold drinks may be harder to absorb initially for some players; see what works best for them.

Recommended food & drinks on court:

1. Cold fluids on each change over to replace lost fluids and cool the body temperature.

2. Sports drinks or coconut water are helpful to replace lost minerals (e.g. salt) and provide energy.

3. Moderate to high GI foods such as: high carbohydrate energy bars or non-caffeinated energy gels and protein digest rapidly are a good source of quick energy.

Discouraged food & drinks on court:

1. Avoid cola drinks or other soft drinks; they usually contain a large amount of sugar and the caffeine may act as a diuretic, which could increase your fluid output and may lead to more dehydration.

2. Avoid fatty/sugary based snacks such as a chocolate candy-bar; they are slow to digest and will sit in your stomach causing a feeling of fullness and reducing fluid absorption by the body.

7.4 Should young players take supplements?

When we are talking about supplements, we are talking about vitamins, minerals, protein and carbohydrates that can be taken in forms other than actual foods e.g. powders, liquids, capsules etc. The supplements we are discussing here relate to legal and government approved supplements.

In a nutshell, if young players are eating a good balanced diet and keeping their hydration levels up, with adequate rest and recovery, they should not need to take any form of supplementation other than a few basic supplements (see below) until they reach the age of 16. Unless prescribed by a health professional.

Supplements that can benefit a young player's recovery, energy levels and general wellbeing are;

1. **Children's multi vitamin** – This can help fill in any of the missing vitamins and minerals they are not getting from their diet. It can also help maintain and boost their immune system (fight off colds etc.) Multi vitamins can be taken orally via capsules, tablets or liquid.

2. **Vital greens** – Vital greens contain a combination of green super foods; foods that are high in vitamins and minerals. They can also be high in protein which helps muscle repair and growth. Vital greens aid in recovery and help keep a young player internally clean. Vital greens with the ingredients: spirulina, barley, wheatgrass and chlorophyll, can be taken in powder, tablet or capsule form.

3. **Magnesium** – Magnesium is a mineral that is readily available and used throughout the body. Magnesium is a vital nutrient that is involved in many important physiological processes including: energy production, improved sleeping, muscle contraction, muscle relaxation and keeping our cells healthy.

4. **Probiotic** – Probiotics are live micro-organisms that exist in the human body. They colonise in the intestines and other parts of the body, including the skin. Where "bad" bacteria invade the body and cause imbalance and illness, "good" bacteria promotes health throughout the body. Probiotics work by competing for space with bad bacteria; they keep the growth of harmful bacteria in check, and stimulate the immune system in ways that help the body recognise harmful organisms. The numbers of each kind of bacteria change, depending on age, diet, health status, and use of drugs (antibiotics) and supplements.

5. **Omega 3** – is obtained from oily fish, which can come as fish oil, cod liver or krill oil. Omega 3's help athletes improve their exercise performance and boost recovery, as well as helping to reduce inflammation and boost lung function during and after exercise.

All these supplements can be purchased at reasonable prices from a health food store.

Once a young player reaches the age of 16, they can look to introduce a protein supplement and carbohydrate supplement into their supplement plan. Proteins aid in muscle recovery and muscle growth, while carbohydrates aid in recovery by refuelling the body. Protein can be taken in powder form, the most readily available and easiest, and there are literally hundreds of different brands. Whey protein is the most common type, derived from milk. For young players, we recommend chickpea protein as it is not as processed as whey protein; it is vegetable based which makes it generally easier to digest. Carbohydrate supplements generally come in the form of gels or powders. They should be consumed during long practice sessions / matches or post session / match.

It is important to seek advice from a qualified professional (doctor, sports nutritionist, naturopath or pharmacist) before starting a supplementation plan for a young player. They will be able to give clear advice on what, when and how to structure the supplement plan. When deciding on a supplement plan, it is highly recommended to source a sports nutritionist or naturopath in your area and get them to assist in the process.

(Over the years we have built a great network of professionals, so if your looking for someone click on the link below and contact us and we can help) http://tennisfitness.com/contact/

8. Young players and injuries

Most, if not every young player, will develop some form of tennis injury during their young careers. Tennis related injuries could be put into two categories; overuse injuries and trauma injuries.

1. **Overuse injuries** – often develop slowly and can start out as mild discomfort that gradually increases and becomes painful. Some common overuse injuries are:

   A – Tennis Elbow – A very common cause of elbow pain, due to the chronic irritation of the tendons on the outside of the elbow.

   B – Wrist Tendonitis – Caused by irritation and inflammation around the wrist joint.

   C – Shin Splints – Pain at the front of the tibia bone of the leg (shin bone). Could be strained tendons, but a stress fracture is also common.

   D – Heel Strain – Caused by inflammation where the Achilles' tendon attaches to the heel bone.

   E - Knee tendonitis – Caused by inflammation of the knee tendons.

   F – Stress fractures – These generally occur in a young player's lower back and lower legs. Stress fractures are bad injuries; the best treatment is rest for up to 6months.

   G – Rotator Cuff Impingement – Pinching of the rotator cuff tendons or bursa (fluid filled sac) within the shoulder joint.

Common injury areas for tennis players
Upper Limb Injuries – 27%
Trunk/back and abdomen - 20%
Lower limb - 40%
Other (thigh, hip, head, eye) - 13%
(from Crespo & Miley, 19)

Most overuse injuries can be avoided; finding ways to prevent them is the key. Making sure young players have the right equipment is important. For example, playing with properly sized and gripped rackets, and using correctly fitted tennis shoes, not running shoes, that give proper support, are critical factors. Always warm up, cool down and stretch after training/matches. Having a good team will ensure young players are getting the right technical advice, which will prevent injury. Getting the right amount of rest

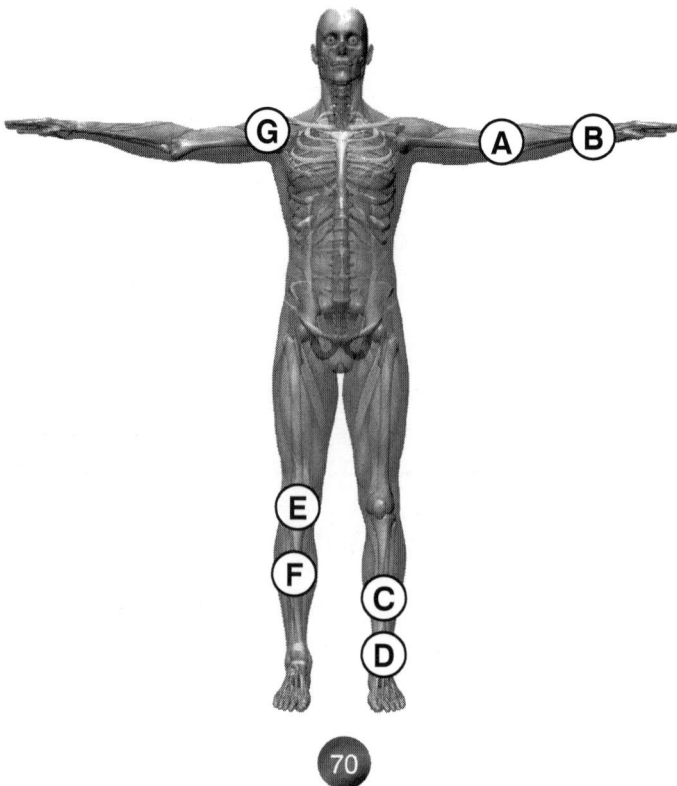

is the most important factor; doing too much with not enough down time, will lead to injury. This is where having a training plan will help the longevity and success of a young player. Working with a structured on court and off court training plan, will minimise the risk of overuse injuries dramatically by: allowing the body to rest and recover, building strength and stability throughout the body, releasing muscle tension and increasing flexibility.

2. **Trauma injuries** – are injuries that occur in an instant. Some examples are: sprained ankle (rolling the ankle joint), falling on court and getting an abrasion and straining the knee (sudden pain in and around the knee joint). Trauma injuries can be scary for young players as they happen suddenly and initially can feel a lot worse than they are; some players may go into shock, feel faint and get nausea.

8.1 How to deal with injuries

If injuries are persistent, for more than one week, it is crucial you get them looked at by a doctor or physiotherapist, particularly if the pain is increasing on a daily basis. In this instance, all training should stop until advice has been given. It is always best to seek medical help from a qualified professional for any injury. During tournaments, there should be a first aid officer available, generally one of the staff members or coaches. Most trauma injuries that a young player will experience will initially be treatable using a basic first aid protocol; RICE.

R – Rest. Try to minimise pressure on or around the area.

I – Ice. Ice the area straight away (20min) to minimise inflammation and swelling.

C – Compression. Wrap the area up using a compression bandage.

E – Elevation – Keep the area elevated as much as possible.

It is advisable to always carry a compression bandage, band-aids, antiseptic cream and a snap ice pack with you. Everyone has different pain thresholds and young players are no different to adults. It is important to know the young player, read their body language, watch their movement and performance, and keep an eye on any general discomfort. Ask questions before mild injuries become chronic. Educate the young player that the best way to treat injury is to first, find out what the problem is, and deal with it in the right manner.

8.2 Foot Orthotics. What are they? And does everyone need them?

Foot orthotics are devices placed inside the shoes, with the purpose of restoring the natural foot function. This is necessary for some people whose natural lower body function has been compromised or is not working as well as it could. Foot orthotics are insoles or shoe inserts; they are generally positioned between the foot and the sole of the shoe. There are various types of foot orthotics and they range in cost also. Most athletes, who need orthotics, commonly use moulded custom-made orthotics. They are moulded and fitted by a qualified podiatrist (foot specialist). Foot orthotics have been used for decades in the treatment of various foot problems. Foot orthotics are used for conditions such as: shin splints, plantar fasciitis, heal spurs, knee pain, bunions, corns, callouses and other foot problems. Foot orthotics can also assist in the management and correction of other injuries and problems throughout the body such as: leg, knee and hip injuries, back problems and postural conditions. In our opinion, it is important to have a consultation with a podiatrist. They will establish if foot orthotics are needed, especially with younger athletes, due to the fact that correct foot function can prevent possible major injuries and the right orthotic can help with that prevention.

Podiatrist assess, mould and fit orthotics. Not everyone needs orthotics and it is important to discuss, in detail, with the podiatrist, why an orthotic is needed, in each case. You need to understand the role they will play and if you feel they are essential for the needs of the individual. We have had feedback in the past, that some podiatrists recommend, or push people, to purchase orthotics when, maybe, they have not been essentially needed, so once again, make sure you feel comfortable with your decision. Foot and lower body injuries are very common in tennis. A skilled podiatrist will pick up on potential injuries that may occur, due to an individual's foot biomechanics. Whether they need orthotics or not a podiatrist will give advice, or a plan, to help prevent injuries from occurring. For that reason, we recommend players see a podiatrist annually.

8.3 What the Professionals do to recover from tennis matches or tennis training?

Recovery can be just as important as the actual training or a match. Having an adequate recovery allows the body to return to a normal state and will help with the physical rebuilding and re-energising the body must go through, in order to physically improve (get stronger and fitter). Without adequate recovery, the body will eventually succumb to injury or burnout.

Below, you will find a list of recovery techniques we use with the professional tennis players we have worked with and how often they should be performed. As with all aspects of on and off court training, it is an individual preference. So find what recovery plan works best for your player and be consistent with it. Note, as young players develop (train harder, train longer, play more matches) so too should their recovery plan increase.

1. **Post match or training** – Run/bike for 10-15 min. This helps to flush the muscle out and can help minimise muscle soreness

2. **Stretch (daily)** – All young players should have an individual stretch plan they follow on a daily basis. This is best done at the end of the day.

3. **Foam Roller** – (every alternate day) Foam rolling is a great way to release muscle tension. It works along the same lines of massage; we like to call it self-massage. There are 4-6 foam roller exercises that can have a direct benefit on young players: Calf release, Quadriceps release, ITB release, Adductor release, Spinal stabilisers release and Gluteal release. They should be performed 2-4 times a week, especially at the end of a tough physical day. (For more information on foam roller exercises, visit our website and check out our foam roller program)

http://www.tennisfitness.com/
foam-roller-programs/

4. **Hot bath** – Hot bath with Epsom salt (1-3 cups) or radox added will allow the body to relax and help alleviate muscle tension and soreness. It is one of the best ways for a young player to relax. Make sure the water is not too hot and spend no longer than 20 minutes in the bath. Do this once or twice a week, particularly at the end of the week.

5. **Massage** – We recommend a deep tissue massage every 2-4 weeks. Deep tissue massage will help lengthen muscle out; release tension and enable better blood flow to muscle. It is one of the best ways to minimise the risks of injuries by balancing out the body and assisting the body to function better. Make sure you find a sports massage therapist and preferably someone with experience. Unless you are use to it, we recommend avoiding getting a full body massage the day before or day out of your match, (unless its treating an injury). Massage can fatigue the muscle and leave you feeling flat and more susceptible to injury for 24 hrs.

6. **Ice bath** – (temperature between 10-15 degrees) either 10min straight x 1 or 1min in ice bath, 1min in hot bath or shower x 3-5 times.

7. **Supplements** – Magnesium, multi vitamin, vital greens, probiotic and Omega 3. Protein powders (if you are over 16 years old).

8. **Hydration** – Depending on weather conditions and sweat levels post match or practice, aim to consume approx 300-500ml for every 1 hour of exercise, on top of your usual daily amount. Coconut water is a great way to rehydrate.

9. **Food** – Foods high in carbohydrates: (rice, bread, pasta), a good source of protein such as fish, chicken, beef and vegetables are best. Some examples are: chicken and salad sandwich, tuna pasta, beef and vegetable stir fry with rice.

9. Tournaments

9.1 Crucial things when preparing for tournaments

When preparing for tournaments, it is crucial to get things right not only for young players, but coaches and parents as well. Below is a list of things that need to be organised before walking out the door:

1. Transport to and from the tournament; you can look to car pool with others

2. Entry to the tournament; check tournament dates and registration papers

3. Accommodation is organised, if required.

4. Time off school has been organised, if needed

5. Check the weather forecast; take appropriate on and off court clothing

6. Always double check you have packed playing gear, rackets, string, sun cream etc.

7. Snacks and drinks: sports bars, fruit, water, sports drink

8. If a coach is going, make sure you have their contact details etc.

9. Any medications or supplements are packed.

10. If you are not travelling with the young player, make sure their supervisor is familiar with any health issues and that they have your contact details, preferably two contacts.

10. Advice from the Professionals

10.1 We asked the Professionals, "What does it take to reach the top 100?"

"There are no shortcuts. Hard work and dedication is important. For me, I always train with a purpose and never just go through the motions. You have got to be prepared to make sacrifices and discipline is a huge part of it as well."

Lleyton Hewitt (ATP Pro player, former world number 1)

"Consistency day in and day out! Doing the right things with the right people around you. Commitment to want to improve. You need to enjoy the journey but be prepared to work extremely hard."

Casey Dellacqua (WTA top 50 singles and top 5 doubles)

"To be a champion unfortunately there is no secrets. It takes years of sacrifices hard work and discipline. You have to have self-motivation and it has to be your passion, it can't come from your coach, parents etc. it has to come from the individual".

Peter Luczak (former ATP top 100 men's player,
Tennis Australia Coach)

"I think the bottom line is that it takes and enormous amount of PASSION to reach the upper echelons of the tennis world. Without this ingredient it will be extremely difficult to sustain the amount of determination and perseverance necessary to over come the undoubted failures one faces throughout the journey.

In today's game you also need to be somewhat of a natural athlete. No doubt you can train and mold talent, however, to reach the top echelons you need to be able to move around the court, you need to get in position to hit the ball.

Once you have the above two attributes, you then need to focus your attention on the mental side of the game. Following my career and after coaching Lleyton Hewitt for two years, I came to realise I was undoubtedly my own worst enemy as a player. I was constantly projecting my thoughts into the future or into the past, this caused an enormous amount of tension to spill into my game. This inevitably disabled my body and blocked what I was trying to accomplish – in essence I was "trying to hard". Once came the realisation that I was my own worst enemy, I asked the question what can I do about this? Then through a combination of yoga teachings, spiritual teaching, and my own experience I have now blended what I consider to be the ideal recipe for unlocking one true potential."

Nathan Healey (former ATP top 60 player and
ATP Coach)

"Tennis is a very beautiful sport but at the same time really tough! It's very self-sacrificing, since a very young age you have to decide you want to spend most part of the day dedicated to tennis, that means you cannot have a "normal" life as other kids, you have to practice hard, do fitness, eat well, sleep well…But the most important thing is to enjoy playing tennis, if you do that you'll be able to do whatever it takes to be at the top.

It is essential to have your parents support. They must encourage you rather than put pressure on you and also guide you throughout the first years of your tennis career."

Nuria Llagestera (WTA top 50 player and
top 5 doubles player)

"To become a top 100 player in this generation requires an incredible amount of accumulated work year after year. The sooner you can develop great habits on and off the court with commitment and dedication the better.

Some days the dream will feel light years away, but if you keep believing and working towards a goal anything is possible in tennis. At the end of the day, its not rocket science, the best players are so disciplined and try to get something out of every training session, every match, everything they do!"

Joshua Eagle (former ATP top 20 doubles player,
Tennis Australia Coach)

"As a player you need a will to win. You need to love competing and to enjoy the pressure situations. Anyone that has ever made it thrives on pressure and the big matches. That's what sets apart the good from very good. As a parent, you need to put your child in the right environment and surround yourself with good people. Every path is different for each child so don't try and compare your child to others or necessarily copy others. Talk too as many players out there who have made it or are doing it (coaches, ex players, current top 10 ranked players in age group). There is no quick way, and no easy way, you have to persevere and be resilient."

Nicole Kriz (former WTA pro singles and doubles player,
Head coach at Newington College)

" I think that the most important things are about mentality and work, the most classic things really, but that's what it is about. Work hard everyday; give everything you have in anything you are doing. Have the will... Believe in yourself, put goals that you can achieve, but that are hard to do and go at them with full maximum fight. Be persistent and positive. Things are always changing for better or worse, always carry on that nothing can stop you reaching your *goals. Have good life balance away from the court in order to have good balance on the court."*

Ceaser Fabregas (WTA top 50 Coach)

"A myriad of factors make a Top 100 tennis player. A comprehensive analysis of the strengths and weaknesses of the player will serve as a guideline to set clear objectives. Developing a solid technical foundation of all shots and movements across the court is essential. Physical aspects such as coordination, resistance, force, and elasticity play a crucial role in a player's performance. However, the only way to get to the top is with a lot of hard work, modesty, passion, perseverance and sacrifice. Attitude is the key to your success. It determines the type of player you are going to be."

Juan Oson (ex player and physiotherapist to
top 10 ATP players)

"To reach the top 100 it takes Love, Passion and commitment. Love for the sport and culture of tennis. Passion for the game, the wins and loses, enjoying the battles. Commitment to build your body and mind, to train every session like it was your last one. Motivation will always be up and down but commitment must always be up there."

Carlos Cuadrado (former ATP player,
Tennis Australia Touring Coach)

"I think you have to have a love for the game and a passion for improvement! Once you have love and commitment then STRUCTURE is the most important ingredient for success. Build a great team and you will reach your dream."

Justin Megraw (former ATP doubles player,
New Zealand coach of the year)

"To reach the top 100 in tennis today you definitely need a positive and supportive team behind you and where everyone with in the team is also working together.

The player has to be clear what outcome they want and when to make definite plans towards that or those outcomes with their teams involvement. They have to be willing to commit time, money and energy into this journey. When things get tough, as they will − not to forget about their outcome (Goal) to help re align them back to their purpose. To help have balance you need 5 different sections.

1. *Tennis − On court*
2. *Training − Off court*
3. *Health (gluten free, wheat free, dairy free)*
4. *Some form of mediation or mental relaxation*
5. *Other activities/Interests/family/friends."*

Alison Scott (former top 100 WTA player)

NOTES

Young Tennis Players – STOP losing matches you should be WINNING!

Get your Tennis Fitness Program

- Move and feel better on court
- Win more matches
- Reach your maximal potential
- Remain injury free

We have trained five 'Number 1' Players in the World

We have worked and trained on the ATP and WTA tour for over 13 years

"And we would love to train you too!"

Because you are a valued client and you have bought this book. Use this code – TNIFTES1 and buy within 7 days and receive a **FREE** – Tennis Specific Warm Up and Stretch Program

Visit this link to get your Tennis Fitness Program and **FREE** Warm Up and Stretch Program

http://tennisfitness.com/online-tennis-programs/

NOTES

NOTES

NOTES

14637430R00059

Printed in Great Britain
by Amazon.co.uk, Ltd.,
Marston Gate.